HBF

HELPFUL BOOK FOR

T-SHIRT DESIGNERS

TeeSpring
Know How

Building Your Own Tee Shirt
Business Today

HOWARD D. EASTON

HBF
EDITORIAL

TEESPRING KNOW HOW
Building Your Own Tee Shirt Business Today

© H.B.F. Editorial, 2014
© Howard D. Easton
   Master Resell Rights

ISBN-13: 978-1500971830
ISBN-10: 1500971839

INDEX

Teespring Reviewed - 5

Is Teespring Right For You? - 6

How to Build Your Own T-Shirt Company with Teespring - 7

Why the Buzz Around Teespring? - 8

Building Your Teespring Campaign It's as Easy as 1, 2, 3 - 10

Learning From the Teespring Platform - 11

Why You Should Have a Look at Teespring - 12

Use Teeview to Determine the Hottest Selling Tshirts - 13

Teespring Uses Social Media to Create Marketing Campaigns - 14

Why Crowd Funding at Teespring Works - 15

Crowd Funding and TeeSpring - How They Connect - 16

How to Create a Successful Ad Campaign for Your TeeSpring Crowdfunding - 17

How to Create a Successful Design to Market on Teespring - 18

How to Create a Teespring Ad Campaign That Works 19

How to Use Social Media to Improve Your Teestring Sales - 21

How You Can Make Money with Your Teespring Campaign - 22

Social Media and Your Teespring Campaign - 23

Using Your Facebook Pages to Make Money With Teespring - 24

Teespring Reviewed

There's been a lot of conversation around teespring.com in recent months, and so we thought it a good idea to have a look at what this site has to offer and why people are getting so excited about it. That's because just about anything flies on teespring.com – it really doesn't matter your reason for selling these t-shirts, although you are certainly going to tell the world so they can decide if they want to support you.

You might be a charity or a non profit with a specific cause. You might have a great idea that you want to bring to market but don't have the capital to do so. You might have just suffered a significant loss, such as a home fire with no insurance and you are trying to rebuild. You might be trying to raise money to help out a person or family going through a medical condition like cancer. The list goes on. What' unique is that the why is up to you.

Crowd Funding

Teespring is a crowd funding platform that is designed to be used by all. You design and sell custom apparel on the crowd funding concept. This means you have no upfront costs. This in itself is what so much of the buzz is around. Once you create your design you send your campaign live and if you meet your threshold or goal, money is collected from the buyers, shirts are printed and shipped, and you get your profit check. If you don't make your goal then nothing happens. No one is charged, the orders are not filled and you don't receive any money. Thousands of people have used Teespring to generate hundreds of thousands of dollars for their cause or their entrepreneurial idea.

Success Stories

Still not sure? Having a tough time seeing how this could make money? Skepticism is a good approach. A few of the more recent success stories include:

* This campaign (https://teespring.com/bunnygirlsings) included the sale of toddler's and children's shirts. The campaign was designed to raise money for an 11-year-old who wanted the opportunity to sing in a children's choir in Hungary.

* Another campaign "Love makes a family t-shirt" (http://teespring.com/chrisandshelleyadopt) was created to help a couple raise money to adopt a child.

* The following campaign (http://teespring.com/staystrongboston) raised over 85K for a Boston relief fund.

There you have it – it seems teespring.com is a site that's worth exploring further if you are looking to raise money for a cause of if you just want to earn a little extra.

Is Teespring Right For You?

The name Teespring might have you thinking about golfing in the spring, but nothing could be further from the truth. This site has absolutely nothing to do with golfing and everything to do with t-shirts and crowd funding.

Teespring.com is a site that allows you to get creative and design your own t-shirt, then market it using crowd funding. Bottom line you could make a lot of money or you could fail miserably. Having a better understanding about Teespring is a good place to start. It will help you determine whether teespring.com is a good match for you and your cause or your entrepreneurial ideas.

Teespring is very versatile. If you are looking to fundraise for your non profit or charity, Teespring is a great choice. If you are running a promotional and awareness campaign, this site can help you. If you are just an entrepreneur who wants to make money, this site can still help you. It's flexible, easy to use, and offers a great deal of potential when you understand the fine workings of it.

You design and create your t-shirt, then you create a campaign and set your goal. In other words, how many t-shorts or what dollar value do you consider having met your goal. If you meet your goal, teespring.com will print and distribute your shirts for you. They'll also quickly send out a check for you. However, if your group misses its target and is unable to achieve it, then no orders are produced or shipped and you forfeit any earnings.

Of course, if you plan to have a successful campaign you are going to have to get active and market your campaign. People aren't just going to find you without a little help. Social media is a great tool to help you achieve your goal. Facebook is especially helpful. You can use your Facebook page(s) to help promote your campaign and you can even take out Facebook ads, which are very affordable providing you understand exactly how they work.

When creating your ad campaign make sure you set a daily maximum budget and a weekly maximum budget. That way when you reach that limit no more ads will run and you won't have any more charges on your credit card either. Without controls, things can quickly spiral out of control. This is certainly one of the most affordable ways to promote your Teestring campaign.

Is teestring right for you? If your goal is to make some money, you don't want to invest any cash and you have some great ideas for shirts then you should give teestring.com a try.

How to Build Your Own T-Shirt Company with Teespring

If you haven't heard of teespring.com, it's time you do. Teespring makes it easy for anyone that wants to create and sell t-shirts to do just that. You simply design your shirt using the designer tools that they provide, then set your price, add a goal and begin to sell. It sounds pretty simple right? What many

aren't aware of is that teespring.com has changed the way in which t-shirts are made – you could say they've revolutionize t-shirt manufacturing.

Teespring has created a way that automates t-shirt manufacturing, which until recently was considered a very labor intensive undertaking. They have also automated the shipping process through the use of custom built software and some developer services.

Evan, from teespring.com says, "I built out an entire admin app for non-technical people to manage the platform...We wanted people to be able to design their t-shirt, launch a campaign, gather orders and tip the campaign, and then have those t-shirts printed and delivered with the fewest possible number of human touch points we could get."

Every day their printers have new jobs assigned automatically. The number of jobs is based on the capacity of each printer. The jobs awaiting printing can be seen in the queue or printer portal.

One of the biggest challenges they faced was the design of an automated system to generate the shipping labels. It's also been a huge 'thorn in their side,' what with domestic and international addresses and the fact that people enter information differently this was a real challenge for Teespring. In fact, for a long time they had a full time developer that did nothing but correct address inputs. But that's all fixed and running very smoothly now.

Evan and Walker met while they were both attending Brown. Evan was a computer science major while Walker was a freelance design and front end developer. They clicked instantly. Some of their earlier endeavors didn't get off the ground, but Teespring, which was developed in their senior year, was different. It was a hit from the very beginning selling more than 300 shirts in the first 24 hours the site was live. Today, it has morphed into something even more. Today many entrepreneurs have discovered a way that they can make not just a little money but a reasonable income. Three's some real potential here and now would be a great time for you to explore this a little further to see what it can do for you.

Why the Buzz Around Teespring?

Recently there seems to be a huge buzz around teespring.com. If you are wondering why, you aren't alone. The answer is – entrepreneurs around the world have been quick to recognize a new opportunity to make money. In fact, if you want to learn the best ways to make money online, then surround yourself with those people that are doing just that.

What is Teesrping?

Teespring is a unique service that lets you create campaigns based on shirts you design, then presell those shirts using their site. As long as your sales hit the threshold you set, your shirts will be printed and then shipped to the customers. Buyers aren't charged until your shirt campaign reaches its sales threshold, also referred to as your goal. If you fall short on your goal then the campaign ends with no shirts printed or shipped and no buyers charged any monies.

You design your shirt and create your campaign and you do this easily within a 10 minute window. Of course, you need to have an idea of what you want on your shirt and how you want it to look. These preliminary steps can take longer. The minimum number of shirts that you can set your threshold at is 10, but the higher you set your goal the more money you will make per sale.

If it is successful, Teespring will pay you using Paypal as soon as your campaign ends and all the shirts are printed. It usually takes only a couple of days after the campaign ends for you to see your profits appear in your Paypal account.

What's so unique about this opportunity is that you do not have to lay out any cash to put yourself into business. This quite literally is an entrepreneurs dream. This all thanks to taking the crowd funding fundamental practices in a new direction.

For a long time, crowd funding was linked directly to charities and non profits, along with others trying to raise money for a cause, such as starving children, cruelty to pets, a specific person, etc. Then crowd funding grew to include entrepreneurial ideas attempting to get their products off the ground. In recent years music and film have also started using crowd funding, so the concept makes great sense.

Teespring is just another venue where crowd funding can be applied in an easy and effective way that allows users to generate income without expenses and at teespring.com it's become very effective with many making thousands of dollars in just a short time. Now that's why there's a buzz around teespring.

Building Your Teespring Campaign It's as Easy as 1, 2, 3

If you have not yet hear about Teespring, it's time you did. Teespring.com is a unique crowd funding site that let's you create, design and sell shirts without ever spending money to get started. So what's the catch? Well it's really pretty straight forward – make your goal you are paid the profits; don't make your goal and you get nothing.

You start by designing a t-shirt. You can use the many designer tools that the teespring.com site provides. Then you will need to set your price. After that you will set your goal (this is how many you have to sell to have a successful campaign) and then you begin to sell. It's as easy as 1, 2, 3.

How can this company do this? Well, it is because they have revolutionize the shirt manufacturing industry. Their system is almost all automated and t-shirt manufacturing until not so long ago was thought to be a very labor intense project. This also reflected higher pricing on these shirts. Now thanks to the automated shirt systems teespring can wholesale to you for much less and that means you can ask less. This typically translates into more sales. You can see why this is a win win for everyone involved.

But teespring.com didn't stop there. They also automated the shipping process using custom software designed especially for them. Thus, cutting production costs even more. It's pretty exciting. Every day new jobs are assigned to the printer. The number of jobs in the queue is based on what the printer is able to handle at that time. Each job is unique as to the amount of resources needed to carry out the job.

Shipping labels have always been one of those tasks that are a bit of a pain. So, Teespring want to automate it, but even automation proved to be a pain, because domestic and international addresses are handled differently. For a long period of time one full time developer did nothing but fix address inputs until they finally got it resolved and running smoothly.

Teespring offers you the opportunity to sell as many or as few shirts as you can in a 24 hour period. When Evan and Walker first started teespring.com they sold more than 300 shirts in the first 24 hours they were open. They knew instantly they had found a winner and they ran with it. Now you get to enjoy those same benefits and the opportunity to make tons of money awaits you.

Learning From the Teespring Platform

Teespring.com sell various styles of tees, but this isn't just any retailer, this is a tee manufacturer that has come up with a brilliant marketing plan that is a win-win for everyone involved. Teespring lets you crowdfund quality custom apparel. It's a simple as that.

There is no upfront costs, there is no risk and there is no hassle. So how exactly does it work? You design and sell custom apparel online by designing your product. Then you sell your product and that pays for the production of your product. Teespring then ships directly to your buyers. That means you don't have to guess how many shirts you are going to need and you don't have to spend your time chasing after cash.

You start by launching your campaign. You use the online designer they provide to create your perfect tee or you can upload your design. There's over 10,000 pieces of clip art in their library. Next, you set your sales goal. So, how many shirts do you plan to sell? This is the minimum you need for the shirts to be printed. Add a description and title explaining your campaign and then start sharing the word. Use Facebook, Twitter, Google+ and other social media outlets to spread your message and tell the world about your campaign.

If you reach your goal Teespring prints your shirts. They take care of all the printing and the shipping and you get paid by them for the profits. This is an excellent way to raise money for a project, a charity, a memorial, or any other reason you want to raise funds.

For example, a couple wanted to adopt and so they launched a campaign on Teespring with shirts that said "Love makes a Family." This was how they planned to raise the money for the cost of the adoption. They then promoted their crowdfunding campaign through their blog and social media. After meeting their goal in just 12 hours, they launched a second campaign.

You can see how it can be a quick and easy way to generate funds. With so many causes looking to raise money, it's easy for you to become a blur in the mix, but with Teespring you can offer a product that interests people and that they want to buy and that makes raising money that much easier than the traditional methods. Why not give it a try yourself?

Why You Should Have a Look at Teespring

If you haven't heart of teespring.com, you should! Here you are going to find crowd funding for t-shirts. Yes, that's right – t-shirts. If you are like most people at one time or another you were sure you had a great idea for a t-shirt. Well now's your chance to take that idea, create your own t-shirt, put it up for sale and see if you can reach your goals and make some money. Let's see if others think your idea was good.

Teespring.com provides users with all the necessary tools to design and create a t-shirt. They also print your t-shirts and send them to the buyer. You handle no product, put no money up front, and do nothing more than come up with a great idea. So what's the catch?

Well, there's no real catch, it's really about how something is marketed and manufactured. Generally, if you wanted to design and market a t-shirt you would come up with your design, then you would get quotes from various manufacturers about the cost to produce the shirt, you would pick a supplier and pay them the costs associated with that order, and of course you would have decide how many to produce. Then, you would market your t-shirts and hope that others liked what you designed because if they didn't you would be out a ton of money. Most entrepreneurs would see that as high risk and they would be right.

Well now there is an easier way, a safer way, that requires no cash out lay, no investment, nor risk. You come up with your idea, you design it on teespring. You create a crowd funding campaign to sell that shirt and you market it through all the channels you can think of. Then you wait to see if you meet your campaign goal.

What happens if you do meet your goal? If you meet your goal teespring will print and distribute your shirts, so still you have no need for hands on the product. If you don't meet your goal the entire thing goes by the wayside, monies are returned to buyers, and you've just learned your idea wasn't maybe as good as you thought. All of this and the only thing you have invested is a little bit of money.

When your campaign is successful, you sit back and wait for teespring to send you your profits check. Now do you see why you need to have a look at teespring.com? You could be missing a gold mine here!

Use Teeview to Determine the Hottest Selling Tshirts

Teespring has become one of the biggest buzz words recently, thanks to the amount of money that it can potentially earn for you. Whether you are a company, a charity, an non profit, an individual, etc. Teespring offers you the opportunity to create and sell t-shirts without investing any money and Teeview helps you to see what's selling and what's not.

Have you always thought it would be cool if you could sell t-shirts with those crazy sayings that just pop into your head? Do you have a cause you'd like to promote awareness for? Are you looking to generate some cash for your charity or non profit? Great news! Here's your chance. Teespring offers a unique crowdfunding opportunity to make money.

In a nutshell, it works like this. You come up with your idea and then design your t-shirt either using the many design tools the site provides or on your own from scratch. Once you've designed your t-shirt you are ready to do some crowdfunding. You decide how many you need to sell. If you meet your goal, Teespring.com will print and ship your orders and then they'll send you a check for the profits. It does not get any simpler.

The trouble is, most of us think we have great ideas and then later find out someone else already had that idea or no one else liked your great idea. That's where Teeview can really help you. On this site you can search to see what' selling what isn't, what's the most popular, what's the most popular for a specific keyword, etc. Teeview gathers t-shirt Facebook and Twitter campaigns for Teespring and then displays this data in one central place.

You can view just those campaigns that are active right now or all campaigns. You can also look at just those that reached their goal, those who have the best selling numbers, and the latest campaigns that have been added. It's handy and certainly helpful. It can help you make better decisions of what product is most likely to be successful.

Teespring provides opportunities that are refreshingly new and simple. If you have a t-shirt idea and you don't have any working capital, it suddenly doesn't matter. Now you can see if the world likes your idea, based on the number of t-shirts you are able to move through crowdfunding. It's a win-win for everyone involved, especially when you combine it with Teeview for some great information.

Teespring Uses Social Media to Create Marketing Campaigns

Teespring.com – if you aren't yet familiar with this website, you should be. Why? Well for a number of reasons. The fact, that this company was able to think outside the box to create themselves a unique niche market, and the fact that this company makes use of crowdfunding, and if that's not enough Teespring has learned to use social media to create marketing campaigns that are successful. Bottom line – most of us could learn a great deal from this company.

You can create a business, build your website and hope that somehow potential customers find you. But the bottom line is that unless you put into place a successful marketing plan, this simply isn't going to happen. The trouble is marketing can get expensive fast. Just look at the cost of Google Adsense and you can quickly see how a small business or a non profit could land up in trouble very quickly. Thankfully, there are other options like Facebook, Twitter, Google + and other social media.

Great, you probably already know about social media and the benefits it can offer, not to mention it's free or extremely cheap if you buy ads. However, if you think all you need to do is post on these social media sites and the customer will come, you'd be wrong. Social media marketing requires you to know who your customer is, who you are going to target, and how you plan to target them. For example, your customer is moms between the ages of 35 and 40 who have children with cancer. You are going to target them through your business page and you are going to purchase Facebook ads to increase your exposure. You are going to crowdfund by creating a tee-shirt that says "Standing up for Childhood Cancer Research,' on the Teespring.com website.

Teespring has plenty of help on their site. The process is relatively easy. You aren't required to put out any money upfront. You create your crowdfunding campaign and if you meet your goals Teespring goes ahead and produces your order and ships it to the customer, then sends you a check for the profits earned. You don't have to handle any merchandise or money.

Teespring knows how to use social media to get the response it wants and you can learn from them so that you too can generate the response you want. Social media is one of the most affordable marketing options available to businesses and non profits.

Why Crowd Funding at Teespring Works

Crowd funding isn't new. There are many sites that offer it and most of you are likely already familiar with the concept. Crowd funding is defined as "the practice of funding a project or venture by raising many small amounts of money from a large number of people, typically via the Internet."

When President Obama passed the Jobs Act it seemed the buzz word of the month became crowd funding. This concept isn't really new, but for many it is a new industry especially for those outside the USA. The ongoing recession has left small businesses struggling to stay afloat and it seems entrepreneurs are also facing some tough times. Crowd funding provides a way for people to have a chance at being successful by showcasing their projects, products, etc. to the world and allowing the world an opportunity to support these concepts.

There are many crowd funding sites available and each tend to offer their own unique spin on things. Rather than having general investors these crowd funding campaigns look to the general public for their financial support, and in many cases they get it!

That's where teespring.com comes in. This is a website that uses crowd funding to sell shirts. Yes you read that right. For tons of people this has proven to be a huge money maker and the opportunity is there for each of us to make some money if we want.

The goal is to create a t-shirt design that you think the world is interested in buying. The site provides you with all the tools you will need to do this. Once you've designed your shirt you will setup your campaign and determine what your goal or threshold is. Then it's time for you to get busy marketing your campaign. Social media, especially Facebook are a great way to do this.

You will also set the time period that your campaign will run. If when your campaign ends you have met your goal, teespring.com will print your t-shirts and ship them to the customer, followed by issuing a check to you for the profits. If your campaign does not make its goal then you receive no money and the shirts are not printed. Those who have ordered t-shirts are not charged until your campaign meets its goal so no money is exchanging hands unless the campaign is a success.

There are few other opportunities where you have the potential to make a great deal of cash without ever investing anything other than a few hours of your time. This is a winning concept, so take advantage of it, because it works. So what are you waiting for?

Crowd Funding and TeeSpring - How They Connect

Teespring.com is a website where you can create and sell your own t-shirts. Crowd funding is simply the collection of finances from backers that are not a financial organization or institute – the crowd – that are willing to fund an idea, a cause, or a platform. So how does a t-shirt company and crowd funding come to be bed partners? Glad you asked, because you'll have to agree that this is a very unique and interesting platform.

Teespring operates by way of crowd funding. In other words, you design your t-shirt(s) and then you create your campaign. Your campaign is based on the rules of crowd funding. You will decide on just what your goal is going to be. Rather than deciding on how much money in donations is your goal, you'll decide the dollar value in sales that will be your goal.

If you reach your Teespring campaign goal then your orders will be processed, your customer payments will be taken, shirts will be printed and shipped. Within just a few days you will receive your check for the profits. However, if you do not make your goal then customer payments are not processed, shirts are not printed and no shipping occurs. You will also not receive a check.

You can see how this is rather a unique spin on the use of crowd funding. What makes it so unique is that it can be used by those looking to fundraise or just as easily be an eager entrepreneur that wants to make a few dollars. Anyone can take advantage of the site.

It's important that you give your shirt design some thought because at the end of the day you need to sell those shirts in order to generate profits for you. If you don't feel you are artistic enough, consider getting someone to help you so that you land up with the very best product you can.

When you getting rolling with your crowd funding you should also take time to pitch your story. What is your organization about, why are they raising money, how will that money help, what will is your goal in order to have a successful campaign. If you are fundraising make sure that you tell potential supporters everything you can to get them to participate.

This is a great opportunity to bring teespring and crowd funding into the same arena. Why not give it a try?

How to Create a Successful Ad Campaign for Your TeeSpring Crowdfunding

You've discovered Teespring.com and are excited about the potential – what it can do for you. If you've never seen crowdfunding like this before, you aren't alone. However, let's be honest – setting up your crowdfunding is always the easy part, but getting people to hear about your campaign and to dig into their wallets and support you, now that's the hard part.

You don't need a fan page to make money through Teespring, although it certainly does help. You just need to understand how buzz niches actually work and how you can find the traffic you want. You also need to understand how you can use social media to promote your Teespring campaign. When you do this correctly, you can triple your sales and it's actually with very little effort, which might surprise you.

Facebook is by far the most popular social media platform to create ad campaigns. You can use your Facebook page and even your personal profile to promote your crowdfunding campaign and you can buy very affordable ads that can help you to expand your reach.

Facebook newsfeed ads allow you to create a highly targeted campaign that will focus on your niche market. If you don't already have a Facebook account you are going to have to set one up. Then you'll need to create a page to represent your company or non profit. Upload your logo, cover photo and say something about your business.

Now it's time to design your ad. You can use an external URL right to your teespring crowdfunding campaign or you can send them to your Facebook page and funnel them over from there. You will be asked to set your goal and then target your audience and who you are targeting. For example, you might be targeting males between the ages of 18 and 25 that play soccer. Finally, you will need to decide whether you are going to do a pay per click (CPC) campaign or a pay per impression (CPM) campaign.

Finally, before you send your ad to live status you will want to review it and make sure it looks and reads the way you want it to. Then send it to live status.

Make sure you set a budget cap on your ads. This is very important, because if you don't you could have a very big bill. For example, set your budget cap for the day at $20. Once you reach that, no more of your ads will appear until the following day.

You can create a very successful ad campaign and help to create a successful crowdfunding campaign on Teespring.com.

How to Create a Successful Design to Market on Teespring

If you have the entrepreneur spirit chances are there's been more than one occasion when you've come up with an idea that you are certain would make money, but trouble was, you didn't have the working capital to get it off the ground. That's where teespring.com is different. Here's a chance to put your ideas to the test without investing a penny. You simply create a t-shirt design that you think will be a success and then use crowdfunding principles to see if you were right.

Bottom line is the design of your shirt. Poor design means you don't get the outcome you anticipated. It definitely a terrific platform for artists to create a revenue stream. The production pricing will vary depending on the design. If you aren't artistic and you still want to create a t-shirt and get in on the action, you might consider teaming up with someone that is.

Don't forget to ask your fans or customers what they'd like to see in a shirt. Post various versions of your t-shirt design to your Facebook page and see what your fans think is the best pick. You will design the t- shirt using teespring's simple to use platform. This includes choosing colors, styles, adding your graphics or text and then tweaking to perfection. You can create mock ups until you find the right combination of graphics and color. You can experiment in a number of ways to ensure that you perfect the t-shirt you are going to sell. Once you have the design you want to use in place, the production of the t-shirt is really quite simple.

Follow the steps to taking your t-shirt crowdfunding campaign live and then you need to be working on your marketing plan. You will need to set the correct tone and think about sending out your message to anyone that is on your mailing list. You can use Facebook and other social media platforms to create the kind of campaign you want and to bring in potential customers. In fact, if you have more than one design and you'd like to determine which to go with try split market testing. It's a handy tools.

Everything you need to create your marketing campaign is available on teespring. You set the goals and if your goals are met then teespring will print your shirts, mail them to the buyers, and then send you the profits check. It really is as simple as 1, 2, 3. Is your idea ready to make you money?

How to Create a Teespring Ad Campaign That Works

When it comes to Facebook and the options available to you to sell goods, the sky is the limit. The site is one of the most visited in the entire world and it is able to categorize its workers so well that you can put your message right in front of the people you want to see it. This makes it very easy to sell just about anything.

When you combine the power of Facebook with one of the favorite online money makers – teespring.com – you are setting yourself up to generate a nice revenue flow. Let's talk about that more.

Teespring is pretty straight forward. You design a tee using their online designer, set your goal, set your price and then launch your campaign. This is where you will send your supporters to buy your tee. Then you'll spread the word by sharing your campaign page. You will collect pre-orders that go towards your goal. Once you reach your goal you will continue to sell tees until your campaign ends. Once it's over teespring will print and ship your shirts and then send you a check for the profits.

That's the basic platform, but you can really take your sales over the top if you use Facebook. If you already have a fan page why not create a t-shirt that fits that niche. If you don't already have a fan page then decide what your designs going to be about and then create a page that fits.

It's important for you to understand how buzz niches work and how to find quality traffic. Create your campaign today and start making money tomorrow. You can have as many campaigns as you want running at one time. For example, November is known as mo-vember for men's prostate cancer awareness. This would be a great time to create a shirt around this buzz. February is Valentines this would a great time to create a shirt around that buzz. You get the idea. You need to take whatever the current buzz is and create a t-shirt that will fit that buzz – that's how you generate money.

In addition, check out the competition before you do anything. Look at what t-shirt designs are working and which are not. You can do this at Teeview. This is a site that shows all of the new Teespring campaigns that have been created and who is enjoying the most sales.

Teespring has created an opportunity for those that can think outside the box to make some serious money. Is that you?

How to Use Social Media to Improve Your Teestring Sales

Teestring is a crowd funding site that uses t-shirt designs as its product basis. It works much like any other crowd funding site except here there's a product involved. You design your shirts, then create your campaign and set your goals. If you sell enough shirts to meet your goal, you make money, but if you don't your campaign ends with no profits for you. Thousands have figured out how to make tons of money on Teestring without ever investing any money. One of the best marketing tools at your fingertips are the many social media platforms. Let's have a look at how you can use them to improve you Teestring sales.

#1 Facebook – This is by far the most effective social media platform at your fingertips. You can post links on your personal page, and promote your campaign on your Facebook fan page. If you don't already have a business page you need to create one. You might also create another page if this is niche market. It can help you to fine tune your potential customers.

#2 Twitter – Twitter is a great little social media tool that lets you send a short message and link to your campaign. You can alternate text and pump out several of these a day to your followers to remind them of what it is you have to offer.

#3 Google + - Many mistakenly overlook Google + thinking it's not of much value. However, it can be. Posting 4 to 5 posts a day is a good place to start. Make sure you include enough text for there to be a good message about your campaign. If it's a fundraising campaign talk about it! What's nice about Google+ is that Google pays more attention to posts here and it can help you to do better in the search engines, which can ultimately help your campaign.

#4 YouTube – Can you create a video to talk more about your campaign. If it is at all possible this is a very good social media avenue to pursue. Take advantage of it. It's free and packs a powerful punch.

#5 Blogs – If you have a blog, take advantage of it in helping you promote your campaign and what it is about. Blogs are great because you have no limitations on the length of your message and you can easily engage your followers.

That's just 5 social media sites that you can take advantage of to promote your Teespring campaign, and for heaven's sake if you aren't familiar with teespring.com now's the perfect time to check it out!

How You Can Make Money with Your Teespring Campaign

If you've heard the buzz around Teespring and the earnings people are generating, your curiosity may have been peaked, and rightfully so. It seems that teespring.com has become the latest how way to make money! If you are wondering how the heck this works and how you can get in on the action, you've come to the right place.

Of course, it all begins with a good idea! Once you have what you think is a great idea for a t-shirt, you can go over to Teeview and see how that fits with what's already out there. You can also take advantage of split testing.

Split Testing is a great way to find out what key ingredients are going to be successful. You can split test for sex, age, area, culture, and tons of other breakdowns. What you test for will in large depend on what your t-shirt is about. Facebook ad campaigns are a great way to test your market, because these ads are very affordable.

Now the key here is that you will want to create three or four different designs and then test each of them to see which generates the most interest and that should tell you what t-shirt you should be designing your campaign around.

When you think you've got the right idea to move forward, you'll need to design your shirt. Once your shirt is designed, it's time to create your campaign and get busy making money.

So how does the making money part work? Glad you asked. It's a kind of crowdfunding. What happens is you design your shirt and then you decide on the parameters that will class it as a successful campaign. For example, you must sell x number of units. If you reach your goal then teespring goes ahead and prints the t-shirts and also ships them for you. Then, they send you a check for the profits. Are you visualizing just why this could be a very profitable venture.

Your only role in the entire process is to come up with a great idea and then design the shirt. After that, teespring takes over. If your campaign is not successful then no shirts are printed and no payments are kept.

The better your ideas, the more money you can make. It's a great way for non profits and charitable organizations to raise funds and it's a great way for entrepreneurs to create an income flow. It's certainly a win-win for everyone involved.

Social Media and Your Teespring Campaign

Teespring is one of the hottest crowd funding opportunities available right now. In fact, it's created quite the buzz. You too can take advantage of the teespring platform and create your own campaign. Then make sure that you put social media to work promoting your teespring campaign.

Social media can be a powerful tool to generate interest for a product or service that's for sale. When it comes to promoting your teespring t-shirt campaign social media can be very helpful. Using your Facebook fan page is an excellent place to start. If you haven't already created a Facebook page now is a good time to do that.

You should also consider creating a relevant page for each niche you are entering so as to immediately target the right people that could be potential customers. Social media allows you to spread the word about your teespring campaign for free or if you like you can purchase affordable newsfeed ads on Facebook.

These ads are some of the most effective yet most affordable ads available. In fact, they are far superior to Google ads, which can be extremely expensive and often don't have as good a targeting ability. Facebook ads allow you to clearly target your market by a number of factors. In fact, you can define your market so clearly that sometimes people actually 'fine tune' their target market too much. Be careful not to do this.

You also need to make sure that you set your daily budget so as not to spend more than you think. You should also set your weekly budget. In this way, what happens is when you reach your daily budget no more of your ads appear and whether you reach your weekly budget early in the week or late in the week, when you do your ads will stop appearing until the following week. This allows you to keep control of your advertising budget.

There are few opportunities that present where you can create a product to sell without ever spending any money. Teespring offers that opportunity. That means that you can actually create a complete campaign without spending a single dime. Remember Facebook ads are optional so you do not need to incur this expense.

When you are looking to social media to promote your teespring campaign don't forget to look further than the most popular social media tools and take advantage of the many others that are out there!

Using Your Facebook Pages to Make Money With Teespring

Teespring offers entrepreneurs a unique opportunity to make money without ever having to invest money. This unique crowd funding site allows you to design, create, sell, market, and ship t-shirts. The crowd funding concept gives this opportunity a unique spin and there's certainly been a great deal of buzz around it. There are a number of ways you can help to ensure your campaign is successful. One of those is by using Facebook pages to make money with your Teespring campaign.

Teespring is pretty cool – in fact, some refer to it as just downright awesome. But really, it's only a small piece of the puzzle. You can design the absolute best t-shirt that's ever been designed using teespring.com and yet not make a nickel if you do not generate the sales. So how do you plan to bring potential buyers to your Teespring campaign? Facebook pages is one of the best tools you have at your disposal, along with other social media avenues.

FP Traffic software is an excellent tool if you want to build and manage a number of different Facebook Pages. Take advantage of the opportunity to create campaigns for niche Facebook Pages then post your Teespring campaign on your Facebook Page. You will be amazed at just how much revenue you can generate in just a short period of time.

Best of all, it will require very little effort on your part. You can use software like FPTraffic to schedule your posts (there are other software programs) and link your shirts to the description and the photo. Most people will spend an average of

4 to 8 hours on a campaign and that's mostly having a look at your stats and just how well campaign is doing.

By building a Facebook audience you can re-launch your Teespring campaigns over a number of months with the same shirts and continue to generate sales and make money. If you have a niche that you can target, even better. Here's a great way to target that niche and spend no money or very little.

Facebook ads can be a valuable tool. They are very affordable and they allow you to target your niche market in a quick and easy manner. Just make sure that you put a cap on your budget for the day and week in total. Otherwise, you can run up a pretty big advertising bill without realizing it.

Plain and simple - Facebook pages allow you to market the t-shirt designs. It's as easy as that.